ME & C(

DIKA AGUSTIN
Illustration by Iqzan Saputra

ME & COFFEE
BY DIKA AGUSTIN

ILLUSTRATION: IQZAN SAPUTRA
(@SYMBOLCULTUREART)
LAYOUT: DIKA AGUSTIN
(DIKAGUSTIN)

for you
who love someone
but don't end up together

a cup of coffee with a strong taste
a bittersweet like our love story
this love, I cannot help
trying to be strong, trying not to fall
I am waiting for you to come home
but darling, you never knock on my door
perhaps it's over and time to move on

contents

DARK

me & coffee

since the day you left me
my light slowly faded

when I notice the shadow of you
all I see is your smoke
and darling, it makes me choke

you are invisible and never be mine
my heart, it breaks
as I still have you in my mind

dika agustin

you poisoned me with false promises
and the new you are a stranger to me
I can't recognize you

seeking for what was never meant to be
and I found your shadow
in the dark theater of my head
however, it only hurts every inch of me

my eyes are too blind to see
that you are a part of memory

me & coffee

the love you gave
made me blind
and the more I think about you
the more I want you back
but I understand
what is broken
will never be intact
I'm bleeding
I want what we have
but it's done, it's gone
it honestly hurts to believe
that you will come home
but not this time
not anymore

I pray I will never wake up from my dream
because the real world never fit in me
I'm out of love without you by my side
never felt so comfortable with the emptiness

– the harsh realities of life

remember what we used to be
and everything was too late
I'm lost without you

I keep running away from myself
it's hard for me to keep my sanity
while I'm too insane
everytime I picture you

I'm half a heart without you
wherever I go
whatever I do
my heart still beating for you
you are the one I want

dika agustin

I'm waiting for you like a cat
lying in a pile of books
thinking about the promise of
a salmon snack that hasn't arrived
you came only to play with
and then you left behind

the unlucky one is my name
I wish I could shut my eyes
and not see you leave
back in my mind
I wonder
I can never understand
how can I believe
in many promises
and ultimately deceived?

– I'm a fool for you

dika agustin

the picture of you
torments me, my head
feelings out of
my control
I wish you can repay
the heartache you caused
it consumed me

me & coffee

too often the fear of losing you
messed me up
now, you're already gone

the new journey
I am too scared of
the unknowns

my soul cry aloud–
not feeling whole
for being here without you
wasn't a dream

and in my own world
I slowly lost in the dark

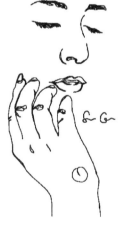

a shadow called love
I stumbled into a lie
where I told myself
I wouldn't miss you
but deep in my heart
I am torn

my brain is uncontrolled
& my soul is wounded
somehow, yesterday's memory
felt so good, yet temporary
now my heart weight heavy
with the fact you are not
here next to me

my world began to crumble
something deep inside me
the silence was too loud
my chest felt heavy
the pain grew bigger
than my body

—the darkness that I face

and the plants and the trees
both prostrate themselves to Him
in order that you
may not transgress balance

the home we dreamed about
has broken down
our pillars are crashed down
and we both collapsed
you hold the power
to shatter me
I never thought you would do it
I watch every single step you take
and you never look back
– *tore me to pieces*

I get everything
like impossible
feels like a waste of time
stays up all night
my head feels so full
yet so empty
has trouble with
the fact that
I want you
the main character
that I miss all the time

(wish you ever come back)

a terrible reality
makes no sense to me
too obsessed with the idea
of you will come home
fall for you
the soul I love the most
yet is untouchable
because I can't reach you at all
loving you is like
a dream come true
but now the dream is over
or perhaps I live in a false reality

I wonder
why real love is hard
for I always get hurt
I guess it's no one's fault
I know I should help myself
before I give my heart away
but it seems hard for me to handle
the broken piece in me

– I want to belong to someone

me & coffee

it's hard to be happy
while holding onto the past
my heart is blue as
I feel your shadow haunts me
in my daily life

suffering from this familiar ache
yet still fresh and new
that grows in me
eating my heart &
my soul alive

ever since the day you left
I've noticed that
there were many holes within

dika agustin

the only love I've ever known is
the one that left me behind
I know that sounds too much
but the heart wants what it wants
I can't blame what has been lost
only I wish I can bring you back

never thought
that would be our last story
and we both ended up like this
how can I see a future with you
while here we are *"strangers"*
to each other?
never thought
that would be our last story
when I hung my hopes on you
when I was too confident
you'd be the last
but the universe disagreed
the two of us were never meant to be

never ever crossed my mind
that you are the one
who gave up on me

I thought to myself
whether I wasn't enough
or too much
or you just couldn't
handle me

like a bird
you fly away
free yourself
far from me

me & coffee

I know the sound of your heartbeat
and it wasn't meant to be mine anymore
I keep missing you
I can't find somebody new

my bed is cold, and I'm lonely
I should have loved you harder before
just to make you stay

the light has disappeared
and this feeling like suicide
my heart dies inside
every time I remember us

dika agustin

our castle crashed down
the darkness surrounded our hearts
there was a war
no peace, no light

anger has no end
no screams, yet silence
slowly, surely
it kills our hearts
and leaving me is your choice

me & coffee

you are mine
and you let me lose
what's mine

when the promise of forever
you've ever made
and like a fool, I believed

our forever is now
we are running out of time
and we both split in two

I wish I won't feel a longing
I wish it won't burn
the petals of my heart

dika agustin

I have so many
words to say
but you are not here
I am longing

when you promised me
you'd never let me go
I know I shouldn't believe it

you took me higher
but when I fall
you weren't there to catch me

and in the darkness
my heart is trapped
by the idea of loving you

me & coffee

I try not to think of you
I try not to miss you
I try to unloved you
but I keep jumping on:
the same feelings
the same thoughts

–I couldn't stop everything

alone in an empty room
looking for the broken pieces
trying to fix piece by piece
there's no hope that can be saved

time is ticking
how long do I have to stay
while everything's like a dream
or maybe I am dreaming?

all the words that you said
stuck in my head
driving me insane
for it still feels like yesterday
it feels so real

if loving you is a beautiful mistake
no wonder why it's disappointing
yet I am too addicted to this pain

and my soul is in pain
since I see my life without you
there is no life at all
I feel completely lost

I should hide all the feelings
behind my eyes and
locked them up inside
as memories always cut me open
every time I think of you

dika agustin

I terrified of love
and every time it comes to you
my mind goes insane

I hate you, but I love you
it's been years since we separated
and I have no idea what to say
I wish we can go back and rewind

I sink into the abyss of memories
drown in pain for holding onto the past
as it's hard to let go of you

now your face all I want to see
and your love is what I want to feel

me & coffee

I won't blame you
even though it's hard to face
the hurt you caused

pushing forward–
hoping tomorrow is
better than yesterday

and sorrow will no longer
be a part of my journey

dika agustin

maybe I will never
have the chance to see that smile
or gaze your beautiful eyes again
remember all your promises
that have turned into memories
and songs you wrote have a melody
but it has no meaning anymore
how can I face reality while
all I see is not clear?
my head is tormented me
because I missed everything
but everything is no longer here
I can't forget you
no matter how hard I try
it hurts me inside

me & coffee

without you
I would be lost
and I couldn't go anywhere
our love may be real
but we can't have forever
sometimes, love isn't enough
to build all the whole world
or even a home for two souls
the saddest truth is that
I'll never be a home to your soul

dika agustin

it's easier to escape
and it's easier to leave
than to stay

I'm sick of thinking about
what did I do that can
make you change your mind

only If I can speak with your heart
only if I can speak with your mind
maybe we won't be here

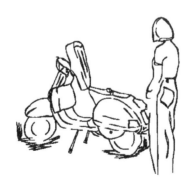

if you come home once more
I'll hold you close
I will never let you go
because falling in love with you
it's such a blessing to my soul
with you, I want to shelter
I don't want to get lost
but I think this must be my dream

– daydreaming

the memories of you
sail around my head
that will not cease
like dolphins
soar through tides
in blue oceans

a sad smile and
a broken heart
I carry with me
as memories of past years
come to my mind

without you
the world is too chaotic for me
but I didn't choose this
it just happened

I'm still trapped
in the past story
trying to ignore
but memories
still holding me back
only if I have wings
I will fly to your home
and meet you to tell you
everything I didn't say

hell for me
since the day you are gone
since you are not here with me
if only I knew you wouldn't stay
maybe I could find a way
or find the reasons
to make you see
to make you feel
to make you believe
how deep my love for you is

me & coffee

did you hear me cry?
I drown myself in loneliness
every time I missed you around
the ghost of you still haunts me
and it makes me fall apart
I have to find a way to hate you
but I can't because
you always be
my favorite lover

we couldn't have
everything anymore
yet memories that
slowly kills me inside
and you, yes you
my one and only
lover who
let me,
myself,
my heart,
my soul
break

me & coffee

I am brain-dead without you
the heart feels heavy
with the pain of losing you
and my eyes bleed out bitterness

I felt the presence of empty space
all over my body
that I couldn't explain
part of my mind was a mess

learn a new language of love
and I name it–
the broken sentences

dika agustin

I saw a part of you
left me bruised
torn me apart
inside my brain
like cotton clouds
cold, dark, and stormy

I felt empty
the heartache
consumed me alive
and tears flowed secretly
broken promises
caused me wounds

unable to protect
this fragile heart
for my lover is gone
blown away
by the wind of fate

me & coffee

I learned not to
show my emotions
but that only
made me drown
on my own sorrow

old feelings
come back at once
just to hit me
my lungs got heavy
there I sink in a sea of tears

dika agustin

the ghost of you
and the loneliness
keep following me behind
I wish our memories
turn to dust
since I can't keep
the pain you caused
I lost and drowned in you
the one who is no longer mine

.

me & coffee

I feel out of focus
every time the memories
hit me back
again and again
– I lost my balance

there is a big hole
and I feel like drowning
deep within

and some strange feelings
beat me up inside
I have no clue
how to help myself
–but cry

you are everywhere
and it hurts my head
what do I do to deserve
all this pain?

–it cuts me so deep

me & coffee

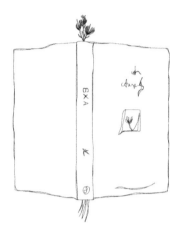

looking back at
the memory book
capturing the image of you
while everything has broken
still struggle to move on
sorrow swallows me whole
tears begin to flow
and my heart feels hollow

dika agustin

how hurtful
holding on
through all the years
but there is a plot twist
on our journey
and torment my heart
and my head
longing, loneliness, and pain
filled my soul
and my heart refused to let go

me & coffee

every time I think of you
my mind goes to
a thousand different places
I know it's all cliche
while all the plots bring
dark thoughts of no tomorrow
a toxic cloud in my mind
a sad ending is all I see
it's my sanity
trying to fight reality
like a nightmare
the fact that I can't
have you next to me

dika agustin

this mouth can't say a word
only a letter by letter that spilled on paper
while my eyes won't let me hide my sadness
and my tears slowly streaming down my face

focus on a paper full of unspoken words
lonely, depressed and overwhelmed
surround the sacred heart

blew up my mind aloud
but the thing is nobody heard

– *absence of sound*

perhaps the pain only looks like a dark room
and there I need your light to shine through me
as I don't want the aches to get stronger
filling up my darkness & my loneliness within

every poem I write
your name is hidden
under my words and
you will not understand
I grieve and cold
you won't be able to
feel my wounds as
I never let you in
and feel my sorrow
let it hurt, it's on me
keep holding on so hard
but I am still falling
let it hurt, let me feel
this heartache on my own
without you knowing
for it is in vain

me & coffee

I killed my ego
just to let you go
fall and feel like dying
driving through the past
on the empty road that I headed

and after everything
you've done to my heart
still, I think you are an angel

trying not to look back
but the space in my soul is vivid
and my heart breaks
my lungs heavy to breathe

I live a lonely life
but the truth is
I don't want to feel alone
I'm so sick without you

dika agustin

crawled back to our history
and the old stories
knock me hard

I surrendered to the floor
I floated, and
the pain grew so strong

your shadow is still
alive in my mind
and my heart is burning
my eyes are crying

me & coffee

I tried to keep
my life back together
my head shaking
for it's hard for me
to bear the pain
I feel half of me is
missing without your presence
and I can't feel a present life
since the day
you chose to walk away
it made my entire world turns blue

dika agustin

I fill your cup till I drained
I fooled myself into thinking
about every moment from the past
makes my heart filled with sorrow
my soul filled with silence
and my mind forgets how to feel joy
like a broken clock
I want to be fixed
to keep me going
and face the future unborn

me & coffee

dreaming of home
that I will never know how it feels
sorrowful but also fills with a hope
a hope that all these things are
just temporary pain

my heart is broken into pieces
for you have left me behind
no matter how hard I try
to glue it back together
it won't be intact as it once was

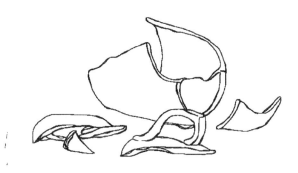

me & coffee

you build a wall
I can't climb
I don't think if you will
let me in again
I don't know how
to get rid of this longing
I don't know how
to take this feeling away
is it a sin
if I don't want you
to leave?
is it a sin
if my heart still
calling your name
or I am just wasting my time
when I know it's all over?

you are not home to my soul
yet, a temporary place to stay
trying to get through my day
pretending to feel alive
but the bottom of my heart refused
trying to give a little happiness
to my wounded soul
but there is a missing part of me
that cannot be found
and that missing part of me is you
what else proves you need?
tell me, so I can fix my mistakes
or am I the mistake itself
and a joke for you?

how can I love you this much
while I only have half a heart?
how can I give all my time and space
only to see you walking away?
how can I feel this hurt and lonely
while I meant to be a solo and hollow
long before I met you?

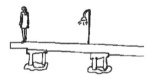

now I wonder why in my mind
I figure you as someone
more than who you really are
and my fault expects you more

– I always see you in good shape

me & cofffee

without a second thought
you pluck those flowers in my soul
my heart no longer blooms
for my root is dying after you leave

–no one nourishes me

the roses you give
slowly die
and each petal falls
like our story that falls
turns into memories

me & coffee

inside of my heart
something broke deep within
the kind of hole
my heart is broken
from time to time
how do I mend
the broken part in me?
I couldn't hold back my tears
and my spirit wept

dika agustin

my happy place began
to crumble to dust
after you left me
and brought the kind of loneliness
my heart cracked a bit
tell me how to mend the feeling
that caused me to suffer
it hurts every part of me
please give back what
you took from me

me & coffee

the petal of my heart has broken
for you never poured me
with your love and presence
I am waiting for the summer dream
watching the season make roses win
while I convince myself
I will bloom without you here
even if it takes a thousand times to heal

BITTER

I am just a sunflower
in the garden of roses
and you might not notice me
for roses are more beautiful perfection
and this sunflower
has a level of vulnerability
the reason why you will never
want to choose me

there is a battle in my brain
I bottle up my emotions
and bury them deep
in the core of my heart

I am torn in two
there between:
the love of my heart
and the logic of my head

sometimes,
that doesn't make any sense
the fear of losing is real

dika agustin

I lied to myself and
tried to resist emptiness
to hide all the feels
I crave toward you
long for your presence
and your absence is
something I can't overcome
long for a world where
nobody puts stones in our path

me & coffee

my world slipped away
on the day when you left
dreams failed
and hopes faded
walk through our stories
that have turned into memories
what a sin it is
for starving a touch
you will never give
I am dying a little more
with each passing day
but why I keep falling for you?

dika agustin

your words are all over my head
running like magical circles
I wonder how to get you out of my mind

I remember your promises of *"us"*
being together, forever
while it sounded like a fairy-tale
for you have forgotten it all
like it doesn't mean a thing anymore

and yes that is true
I hate the idea of remembering you
it drives me insane

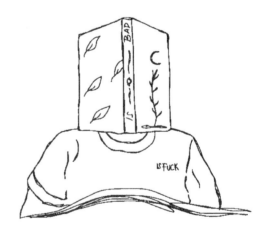

me & coffee

I am no longer the reason
behind your heartbeat
and that makes my whole world
turn to grey
I'm broken, lost, and far from sane
because of your face stray in my head
searching for a way
to get rid of my feelings for you
but still, you are the answer

–darling, wish you were here

looking out through the window
I see the sky begin to cry
inviting me back to the ancient pain
I grieve when I remember your figure
and I can feel the heaviest in my lungs
every time I inhale the air
I wish you were here
to fill this loneliness zone

me & coffee

I've tried to understand and
tried my best to hold on tight
to make you mine again
but the more I try, it just bleeds me
maybe I should let go of you
or wait until all these feelings fade
knowing this only brings me down

bottle up all the feelings
inside my chest
like a missing puzzle
I lost a part of me from my soul
when we no longer say hello
you seem to enjoy
the unspoken word
and the idea of you would
come to rescue me
messed me up
darling, you are too
comfortable without me
and here I am shattered

me & coffee

a warm feeling pierces
through me every time
I listen to a song that
reminds me of you

the magical tone let me wonder
all the things about you
and a natural rhythm
in my heart and my soul

here I feel your presence
in my loneliness

dika agustin

all of me yours
but then you fade away
separated from me

I never thought it would be so easy
for you to slip away from my life
as if it meant nothing to you

grieving, I am now and forever
struggling to be happy as
the universe isn't mine
when I'm not yours

me & coffee

there is no way
to escape –
no heaven
but hell

you let me
wander
insane

my thoughts
stumble upon
you
and the pain
swallows me
whole

there are no more us
as our dreams together
are disappearing
I feel your love
crawling out of my heart
falling to pieces
my mind lost between
the past and present
I held my breath and
count to three
begging and praying
not to turn around and see
what was behind
no more running around in circles
the wheel has broken
I won't ask
I want to erase memory
in my mind
and leave it all
let it in the dust

me & coffee

the weather
was pretty windy
from inside my window
I see a dark sky
crying for help
spilling every name
through the rain
and your name is one of them
falling to the ground
nowhere to be found

dika agustin

longing for your touch
and this feeling isn't
for the first time
the thoughts of you lead me
astray in my mind
I still picture you
like the beautiful figure
or is it my head too beautiful
to think all the best in you
for I couldn't see your imperfection
after you left me to suffer

me & coffee

every thought
  goes to you
  the future we hold
  no longer for us
when I dream
  to grow
  something beautiful with you
  but turned into nightmares
we flip up like upside-down
  today we are gone
  we walk on our own

dika agustin

when I go deep into my mind
every memory guide me back
into the place where
I buried all my pain
while my heart slowly mends
I hope your shadow dies
so, I can look into a good life
without feeling dumb
for the rest of my life
by thinking of you
thinking of seeing you soon

me & coffee

I am looking for more and more
the right word to say
yet, there are a million words
I couldn't spill it out of my mouth
my words left unsaid

the same narrative
feels so familiar
and it never gets old to me

my vision is getting blurry
slowly fade
I can't feel anything
at the moment
I'm numb

every time my phone rings
I hope that is your name
that appears on my screen
and says–
"hi, do you miss me?"

me & coffee

with my eyes open
but why is it still blind
to see the truth?
falling apart ever since
you slipped out of my sight
you paint my whole world
with gray and blue colors
when I want you in my life
but the time makes you fade
and I vanish from your sight
now I am a silhouette to you

dika agustin

the hollow space
fills up my chest
whenever I remember
how you turned me down
you go wherever you go
and choose what you believe
my love is no longer your side
and it messed my heart

me & coffee

a forehead kiss
from you warmed my soul
and in your arms
you made me feel home
but now everything has changed
the nightmares between
my world and my fantasy aching me
you aren't here with me
what's left are memories
that fill my mind like hollow spaces
your promises burn to ashes

dika agustin

all I want is to be your lover
the love of your life
because of every time
I'm around you, I'm home
and your eyes are heaven on earth
but the truth on the other side is
that I mean nothing to you

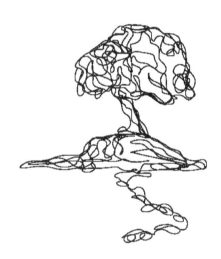

why is our story temporary?
I thought you would come back
but I would not give up hopes
even though I have to
love you in silence

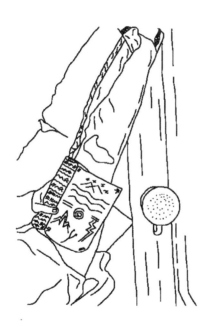

dika agustin

I miss the morning rain
and the moment where
you are still around
how your presence
could recharge my soul
so, I can go my day
with happiness
now, I crave the feeling alive
when you are around
but I keep stumbling and
get caught into an idea of
you everything to me

me & coffee

a cup of cappuccino
black and white represents
the color of my soul
with a strong aroma
I drink and let it
run through my body
it tastes bitter-sweet
like the love
you've ever given

dika agustin

I miss those starry eyes
when you gaze me deeply
when I see you speak
but my brain stops to think
because I drowned in you
too often, I think
about those moments
my bad that I wish
I could go back and
be with you again

me & coffee

you are the black coffee
no cream or sugar
I like you even if
you give me
dark
bitter
love
pain
you are the caffeine
I am addicted to you
consumed me
now I don't know
how to help myself
from this feeling

dika agustin

I pour milk to
your cup of coffee
to give a flavor
but in return
you pour salt in me
you create an ocean
in my heart and
guess who is
drowning?

me & coffee

like ice cream that melts at me
you taste so sweet and make me
want you as you are
always my obsession

don't tell me if this is too much
because you make me feel this way
until I don't know how to undo
all my love for you

when you leave
you also take a part of me with you
and you will never give it back

you said my wishes
are the command
flying me to the moon
how innocent, and foolish I am
for I believed the lies you give
the words you spoke pain me
(deeply)

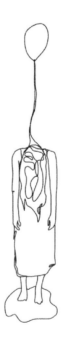

me & coffee

there is
a morning
inside you
waiting to
burst open
into light

dika agustin

what the hell do you want
break my heart again?
you cut me open
poisoned my blood
you said you would stay
but you changed your mind
you had your direction to go
you said it fits you
and leaves me no choice
but let go, leave me numb
hard for me to believe
that us is history

come to
rescue me
I fall, and
all I need is you
a piece of my heart
hard to see you go

dika agustin

the line of that song
you wrote for me is
still in replay mode—
stuck in my head

you call me sweet baby
home to your soul
but everything is gone

you built a vision for
my whole world
but there is also the darkness
that you create

tell me how to believe
I blinded by your lies
yet it tastes so sweet
and somehow
my heart can't deny it

me & coffee

I've read many books in my life
but my favorite is the one
I pen down for you
a story I didn't say
after you left
sad, but it's true
that I keep re-reading
to remind me of you
even though
the ending isn't
beautiful

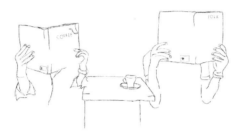

you are the storybook prose on the pages of my book, I could go back and reread with an infinite number of pages. every paragraph that never ends, the story is filled with sweet memories of us, but these narratives mean nothing to you. in the last chapter, you ripped my pages, separating us forever.

me & coffee

how can I forget
while every part of you
is still alive within me
am I just wasting my time?
— *asked my inner-self*

I don't think if we can
get back together
I am still offended
by how it ended
but I try to understand
even though it isn't easy
to replace you
missing you is hard
and your absence
incomplete me
honestly, I have no idea
what's the point of
looking back if
that only hurts
every inch of me

me & coffee

I was too naive to love you
I couldn't see clearly
which right, and wrong
because I was too afraid
to lose you
until the universe
decided our destiny
and here we are
both of us are
no longer together
but I can't seem
to vanish this feeling
I love you too much
I love you like a child

time has frozen
yet, this heart longs
for the familiar feeling
I used to feel
when I was
with you
no more eternity
for it filled with
a world of memories

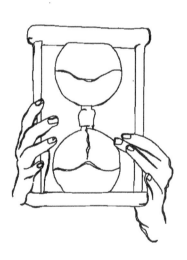

me & coffee

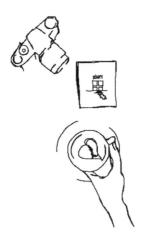

capturing you
on a blank paper
of my diary
as I can't get
to see you anymore
wondering how
to wash away the pain
so, I write it down
for this heart can't
bear the longing
crave for love
that is no longer
mine

dika agustin

because of this heart heavy
and it's okay to feel vulnerable
these feelings are hard to handle
I couldn't hold tears
the mind was hollow
I was drained by someone
who incapable to love me

me & coffee

what I learned from loving you
is not only about giving
but also damaging me as a person
and it's so painful

losing my sleep
and always stay up at 3 am
the thought of you
is too strong, haunt me down
that was me, crying, and
causing my breath
to come out shaky

I was able to get up
also just because of my mind
and my body was tired
falling apart from losing you

only if I knew how
to save my heart before
perhaps I wouldn't
be broken like this
or put myself in danger
only to catch you

me & coffee

my best mistake
is to let you in
and give more chances
while I should never
let you come back or
say hello again
yet, leave you behind
like the way you did
but I guess I'm too naïve
to believe in you once again
that you've changed
I realized I was too afraid of
the separation that made me stayed
with a bleeding heart

–it was my fault

I regret thinking that
I wasn't good enough for you
I changed into someone
who wasn't me
for you didn't accept me
as a whole
you wanted me
to be someone
who I shouldn't be

me & coffee

you paralyzed me
with your lies
yet, tasted so sweet
like honey that dripped
and filled the space inside
warmed my lungs
but it was a temporary feeling

I didn't mean being harsh
but you did break my heart
I lost myself while saving you
I drained to meet your needs
and I became friends with
the chaotic you caused

but it's time for me to leave
because you couldn't see or realize
what you did torment me
so I'll save myself

when that day has come, I have no more time to give as I realize you won't be returning; so, I'll keep on walking like I don't need you as you don't need me. you burn my heart, and I have no title for this feeling. perhaps, this is the pain of loving you, the misery I go through where you put me in a line between love and hate at the same time. now, my heart and my soul say goodbye to you for good.

change is painful
hard to face
but I have to
maybe, leaving is
a better choice than
staying and living
with someone
who doesn't see my worth

—I let go with grace

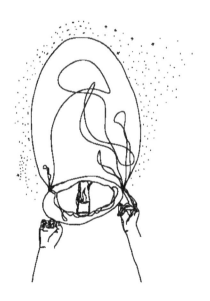

the absence of your love
doesn't scare me anymore
and I don't feel strange at all
I even made a funeral
for the broken you caused
as there's nothing
could be saved
but let go of
what we had
and bury them
deep inside

me & coffee

I used to feel fearless waiting for you
but I thought I was too blind
because too in love with you
until time slapped me with the truth
opened up my eyes that I am enough
to live my life without you

dika agustin

I let all my hopes
about you collapse and
the hardest season of
my life is walking away
creating space to grow
into a version of myself
yet, feels so strange
I became a stranger
but I understand
my love cannot be
created or destroyed
only can be transformed
where I will finally accept that
losing you is not
the end of my day

me & coffee

I thought I was home to you
but the reality hit me
when I knew the fact that
you treated me like
I am a hostel
to your soul
and you are
a visitor
in my life

dika agustin

it's true I don't have
to try harder
just to make
this relationship works
or prove to you
if I am worthy of
your affection
while you don't see me
and this one-side love
better for me to end it

perhaps
I was brave enough
to move on and face the day
hoping for reality
because this is not a movie
get away from tomorrow's trouble
as I want to live a present life

there is no need to feel lonely
I'll sail away from this broken heart
because I realize my time
on this earth is temporary
and I should live my life freely
I will no longer chase you
I won't push myself away
to fulfill my desire
to be with you while
you don't choose me anymore
and this complicated love is us
and I set us free

me & coffee

time may be different
probably it means
for the future

let the
beautiful things
of the past end

people come and go
two of human hearts
don't beat as one anymore

I'll spread the wings
for I am ready to fly
and find a safe place to stay

with you I experienced
emotional violence
and thoughts that led me
to inner conflicts

having a human experience
such a broken
it was tough and challenging
until I finally found my worth

I am better off without you

even though a part of me gone after the day you left, I stopped relying on you to complete me. and somewhere farther away, I'll get there in a safe place where this pain will heal, and my heart will be whole again with or without you.

to be my own safe place
I must live far away from you
mending my wounds
and not depending on you
to fix my dying life

my past seems hard to bear
when everything always
brings me back to you
my job is not
to let my ego win
nor not to let myself be
a prisoner of the past
I have to move forward
without a doubt

dika agustin

for you the one who
gave me a heartache
goodbye is all you deserve
my heart might shatter
but it doesn't mean
I won't get better
let these feelings be here
I won't punish you
I forgive you
for my own sake

me & coffee

my love for you
as deep as the ocean
but I must swim as
I don't want to sink
in the dark and cold

you break my heart
and now I break mine
by giving up on your love
not because I unloved you

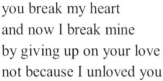

only somehow
to save myself from drowning
I have to save myself by keep swimming
because I no longer wait for you
to save me with your broken ship

from now
I know happiness
doesn't start with you
I believe you are
an impermanent pain
and now I want
to fall in love
with myself again

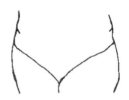

SWEET

me & coffee

the most
important thing right now is
to stop killing my heart
by being sad and
stop wasting my time away
by being unhappy over things
that aren't in my control
at some point
letting things all go is
better than holding things back

dika agustin

I need to come back to reality
I won't let the thought of you
travel in my mind
I won't let the pain you cause
under my skin
I won't let the thought of you
rip me apart
I won't let the thought of you
stop me from moving on
never again

who is not a selfish human being? I was a selfish human being who is holding on to someone who doesn't want to belong to me anymore. I was a selfish human mind that thinks I can bring back what has been lost. I was a selfish human alive who is emotionally in pain of waiting and staying. I wasted my time, my energy, but it was the old me, a selfish me. I won't hurt myself the way I did before, I learned to appreciate the human in me since I do believe I deserve the purest, the rarest, the unconditional love, and I do believe everything is in the right place, the beautiful things are coming my way.

dika agustin

things are different now
when reality slaps me
telling the truth in life
like a dagger through
my fragile heart
and left me broken
but the thing I know is
that all exists for lessons
I can learn to begin
a new journey

when things have
drained me down
there is a song that
can bring me back
to reality

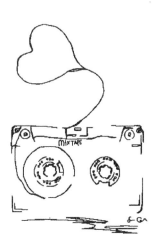

a song that
can walk me through
all the fantasies

a song that can
make me forget
all of my misery

a song that can
pour magic
into me

a song that can
bring warmth to me
my every tomorrow

even though I love you
that doesn't mean I will
let you hurt me and reopen
my wound once more
if I let you be the scar
on my heart that
because to remind me
how hurtful it was
and to remind me
that it's impossible for me
to take the same road to go
and if I don't try
I will never know what
will happen in front of me
so, I walk away and let go of
what I couldn't control

me & coffee

sometimes, it's better off alone
than being together with someone
who doesn't want to see you win
makes you live in a cage of the mess

sometimes, it's better walking away
than walking nowhere
stuck in the same place
where you can't grow

sometimes, it's better telling the truth
than fooling yourself by
saying someone will change

sometimes, it's better off alone
and changes on your own
than stay with someone
who doesn't want to change
and grow together

and by letting go
I found love and freedom
I finally found myself
and each end was
just a new beginning

yesterday was gone
and tomorrow is
what I need to face
why am I being
so worried about
what has gone
instead of living
the present life
peacefully?

when was the last time you told yourself to do things that made you feel at peace? I guess you forgot that as an act of self-love, self-care, and self-respect in life, you must invest more of your time in yourself, you must sink into your inner-self get to know what you want, what you need in a case to set boundaries. so, nothing can defeat your soul when they do harm you, you know how to save yourself.

– what my heart needs to listen

me & coffee

the heart of mine
grows stronger
no need to depend
on other people's hearts
to feel happiness as
happy on my own is
my purpose

even though
someone and time
kept pushing me away
but I won't blame
or complain
I forgive

for love is where I born
and love is where I belong
I'll make amends on my own
since I deserve no fear
I deserve peace

dika agustin

maybe right now
my journey is about healing
giving myself permission
to take a space and
take care of myself
on my own

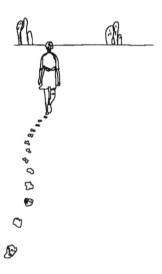

maybe right now
my journey is about
having hope
letting myself believe
that I deserve better

maybe right now
my journey is about
being home to my soul
giving another chance
to reclaim my joy
and be who I am

perhaps, I was too innocent to believe in love and blinded my eyes until unable to see the red flag. perhaps, my expectation toward you was too high, caused me the heartbreak of betrayal, disappointment, and abuse of trust. I don't feel my well-being and beat myself up since I wasn't feeling good enough, just because you abused my heart. I think I am responsible for the pain in me because I let you in. I needed to forgive myself as a part of a human being. I am my own mistakes, I need to learn and take horrible experiences as lessons. I shouldn't beat up or punish myself, but more forgive and embrace as I won't grow, I won't be mature, and even stronger if I didn't cross those paths. I know my cup is empty for I was giving all to you, now my job is fulfilling my empty cup with extra awareness, extra self-love, and extra self-care that nobody could ever give and responsible for how I feel, but myself. I need to get back to who I am meant to be and reload my energy, no need to focus on what hurts me, and just want to see myself free, feel peace.

dika agustin

I looked back and realized
how simply brave I am
to leave the past behind and
fall in love with myself again
at some point
being alone isn't
a sad story

me & coffee

I know I wasn't born as
a broken human being
only someone in the past
put me in a hard situation
caused me broken
and have a heavy soul

yet, I chose to run with the wind
let it took me and led me
to set me free from the suffering
in hope, the strangest feeling goes away
I want to feel whole and holy again
like I was born

dear myself
it's time to wearing
your heart like a crown
you are the queen
with or without a king
you are enough
no need to pretend anymore
your body is your kingdom
you are safe here

me & coffee

even though there are
many reasons to be sad
but I do believe there are still
many chances and
reasons to be happy
and be grateful is what
makes me stronger
I think it's bold
that I choose
to begin again
to fight
to hope
to love
to live

dika agustin

I was lost and found
all at the same time
there is a part of me that
I can't recognize, and
that is the old me

my brain was on fire
burning my fears
I am not afraid
I don't want to be a prisoner
of my own mind

I was born free
I won't let a broken heart
take my life away
nor let me suffer

I am unstoppable
racing on my own

me & coffee

when I feel like I don't deserve any
I try to embrace the pain
allow myself to meet my needs
to take care of myself
to practice self-care
and self-love
when I'm hurting
sometimes, all I need is me
being kind to my own self
and to let the burden
fall down

how many times have you let someone
break your heart with inconsistent love?
how many times have you let someone
occupy your throne and take your land?
how many times have you let someone
destroy your kingdom?
take back your land
rebuild your kingdom
claim it yours
and never let anyone
harm you, not again
please, rise instead of grieving!

–heart to heart talk

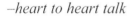

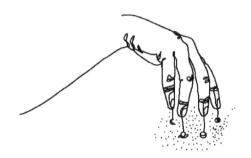

when I focus on the hurt, my heart will continue to bleed in a broken situation. my brain goes to the dark side, but I have the power to control, to choose which road I want to go. I have that ability to change, I may be in pain, but I am not fragile. I am a gentle soul, my heart is so pure, and I use it to forgive them who left and hurt me, to forgive myself and my mistakes. the wise thing I can do is learning to balance my ego instead of complaining or forcing myself to stay in the broken line.

dika agustin

thinking about the reality
of the future without you
breaking my heart
I thought what we had real
and last forever

but I know that what isn't mine
will never be mine
your name wasn't written for me
I expected a lot and it hurt me
the fact is that you've left me
somehow, I must be strong

I won't burn our memories together
but I let time erase you from my mind
and I let time be a healer of my aching heart

life is not always a sunny day
even sometimes the sun can burn
life can be pouring
but there will be
a rainbow after the rain
I must remember to breathe
and I must try to live
through pain

remember when beautiful things end just let it be, don't grieve deeply. sometimes, you'll experience things you don't want to experience. sometimes, fate is unfair because the ending doesn't end up the way you wanted to be. sometimes, you need to understand, and accept it even with a heavy heart. sometimes, the reason someone leaves is that because they want to see you win with or without them by your side. however, that's their decision, they have their own reasons or perhaps, they hurt too, and have their own battle you never know. I know you may disagree because it doesn't make sense in your logic, but it is what is. sometimes, the ending has to be stormy or messy, but at some point, you are the lucky one. you'll experience new things, new life, new journey, you'll grow after it all. – reminder to myself: *you grow from what makes you suffer*

me & coffee

I can't travel
into the past
I let my guilty asleep

I forgive myself and
give another chance
because everything
happened for a reason

leave my troubles behind
I know it hurts that
people come and go
like waves

so, I set them free
and let go

dika agustin

time will go by
everything will get better
I know that I deserve more
remember, I will not die
from suffering
for I am a survivor
I will survive
I will grow and
I will transform
into the person
I never could
imagine before

– I will laugh, I will live again

me & coffee

I was never too much for love
I only gave it away to the wrong one
from now on, I'll be careful
yet, I am not afraid of love
as I do believe the love I deserve
will see my worth
will accept my imperfections
will love me unconditionally
even when I'm not at my best
nor when I think like I don't deserve it

dika agustin

you are not the glue
for the broken pieces
yet, it's me who holds
the broken pieces
back together

me & coffee

I can't explain
how my mind runs
but what I know is
my troubles seem
to fade away

the home within is
filled with joy like
my life begin again

I am alive and
every breath I take
no longer wasted

hello, my soul
welcomes home
time to love myself
until time runs out

dika agustin

sadness slowly came out
only a little space but
now I know how to manage

I thought I wouldn't survive
for I was trapped in
a labyrinth of my mind
here I am, free of fear

I breathe my freedom
all my heart, and my life is
in a one rhythm again
the broken girl no longer
my middle name

the unfinished stories
I left them behind as
I started a new page
and I am more than fine

when everything feels wrong
remember it's okay
to press the pause
free your mind
and breathe, live the present life
you are still alive
and know that even in every crack
there's a flower can grow
and ready to bloom

–self-talk: a wildflower

dika agustin

I was letting myself
locked in an emptiness
now, I will take
my broken wings
and fix them
I will learn to fly
through the darkness
to see what I'll find
if I'm lucky
I'll reach the sky

me & coffee

in all of the experiences
the highly important thing is
that everything makes me
who I am becoming
whatever I do, I have limits
and I know I have had enough
my purpose is to continue
to live this life and
can smile out of the blue

dika agustin

the holes that left in me
made me feel bittersweet
and I fell apart only
to keep you close
slightly mend my broken heart
it's time for me to go
through darkness and pain
I'm going out of my blue world

I've never felt so loved
until I saw what was inside of me
I found the secret-self
an unconditional love within

dika agustin

there are dark corners of my mind
this is my responsibility to choose
my choice is giving the light itself
trying to explore to find my way
as I don't want to stay there
live in the darkness

turn on your music so loud
dance my dear

through the tears and pain

dance my dear

let's have fun, let's create the joy

dance my dear

let your body sink into the melody

dance my dear

free your sorrows

dance my dear

everything will get better

dika agustin

dear heart
don't let the
pain consume you
or bury you deeper
or come and get you
you aren't dead yet
come out of your grave
breathe the fresh air again

in this body
I do believe that
this is the right home to stay
a safe place to shelter
I hope loneliness will
fall asleep

there is no time limit for happiness, and good things must grow. I need to check the reality that beauty is in me, not what others can make me feel. since I'm done chasing temporary things and I am no longer search for forever, I only want to live today's life like there is no tomorrow and love myself with my whole heart.

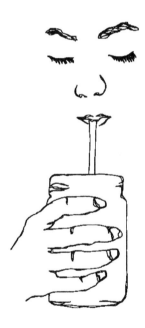

me & coffee

I draw my heart first
find the balance before
other heart's pull me in
reminds myself that
I have to love me first
before I give my heart away
for I understand no one
can fix the broken in me
no one can complete me
but myself

dika agustin

I run away from you
until my legs go numb
I can't risk myself at all
and look like a fool
for one-side love

I can't sit with pain
that's why I choose to run
I don't want to look back
I keep moving on
and even if I have to face
the empty moments

I don't mind
being alone with myself
keep my own company

me & coffee

I have a reason
on this earth to be happy
being able to live
to make this life simple and easy
that is exactly what I want
and who I want to be

dika agustin

maybe it's weird, strange, and scary
but there's nothing more wonderful
than healing on my own
I can't believe that I can get through it
I can't believe that right now
I am in a stage of life
where I can feel happiness
and no longer depend
on anyone, but myself
I can't believe that I am alive

me & coffee

I might miss
the opportunity
but I am not left empty
all that was lost was
all that I gained
and deep longing is
no longer here

thank you for
my mistakes
from you I learned
how to give myself
a chance, and permission
to change my pathway
to find my human soul

dika agustin

it took me years
to figure out my heart
to figure out my mind
and to figure out my soul

it took me years
not to hold back and
learn to let go

in order
to grow
to heal
to survive
to feel alive

me & coffee

every heartbreak has been
only one step forward
into the person I am becoming
sweet time will let me meet
the gentle version of my pure heart
at the highest level
because who I am today is
a different person from
who I was yesterday

dika agustin

nothing to regret
nothing to expect
like petals
everything can fall
but it doesn't mean
you can't grow

always remember your roots
don't be hard on yourself
nourish yourself
give yourself a chance
to bloom again

I hope you find the courage
to come and to look at love within
I hope that love gives you strength
and let it heal all the scars
throughout your whole body

– *I forgive myself*

me & coffee

in every losing
I try my best not to blame
I learn to accept what is lost
I try to keep my head up
when all the things
about to collapse

I can't force my heart to wait
and serve your return
after you leave me
as I have nothing
to hold onto anymore

I choose to walk away
I don't give way to hate
and I forgive

and sometimes to keep
myself back together
I must break my own heart
by letting go of
what I love the most
yet, I do understand
in the end, it's worth it

my lonely heart :

there is nothing stopping you
from trying to find a place
you mean to stay
you are too early to give up
you are too young to die
just breathe and live
you deserve it

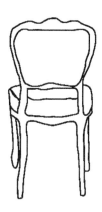

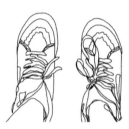

somewhere between love and hate, somewhere between keep walking or keep staying. how will I ever know if I will find love again if I don't go?

we were good together
but now I am too good
to be apart from you
growth and change are
something I dream before
and I'll go out there
I'll go on my way
I'll bring home
once more
to my soul

dika agustin

let yourself feel that
even though you must
experience dark emotions
this life is not always
about happiness
life is not a disney

somehow, you need to learn
how to deal with those feelings
in the healthiest way and
understand that feeling is temporary

remember
you are capable of healing
you are capable of being happy again

–I give myself a chance

through the breaking
comes my faith, and
I am the keys:
I am the key to my love
I am the key to my savior
I am the key to my heal
I am the key to my future
I am the key to my destiny
as I am whole since begin
broken is not me
not my name

dika agustin

one day, I'll find a home
without a roof and
makes me feel safer

one day, my loneliness will pay
I'll smile again and
the only thing left is joyful tears

here I am just trying
to heal myself
from people
from the situation
from the bloody life

me & coffee

I sit in the middle of the night
talking to the moon
wondering how I carry on without you
I guess that is true
time heals all the wounds
changes me into someone new

dika agustin

a sense of hope is
still beating inside
knowing this little soul
feels the sparkle of joy
my heavy heart and
my cloudy mind
both are relieved
my entire world
has changed

I see life

me & coffee

today is a lot better
as the sun comes up
with the beautiful sunrise
it seems like the light
comes up to me
brightening
my darkest day

dika agustin

enjoying a cup of coffee in the morning
sitting alone under the clear blue sky
feel the breeze gently kiss my skin
and yellow sun is my happiness
gives the light to my darkness

me & coffee

I forget about you
the pain in my heart
gets better day by day
the memories
slowly fade away
my bruise lungs
are no longer blue
and every breath I take
no longer hurt

I was black and white before you, but then you colored my soul like a rainbow. my whole world was beautiful, for you painted me with all the colors. sadly, the colors fade as you left me too soon, but now I am the blank canvas ready to paint new colors all over me, with the most amazing hues, without you.

me & coffee

freedom is in you
you have the power
to set yourself from sorrow
listen to the drums of your heart
let your emotions flow
like water washes away
your sadness, your fear
go, sweetheart
walk gracefully and rise
unlock your cage
and live your freedom
you deserve precious life

– my inner-self knows better

dika agustin

I have the love that lives within
it's so wide, so deep,
and true that happiness is simply
coming from within
flowing through me
filling the hole in my soul
with beauty–
I am soft
yet not weak
I am kindness

me & coffee

and self-love is
the glue to keep me
sticking my broken pieces
back together

this book is inspired by
many people and things
in reality around me
the good or the bad
I am grateful for
the experiences
the memories
and the lessons

to the readers:
I thank you for supporting me
being a part of my journey
you make me feel exist and
words would never be enough
to express myself and
how much it means to me
I hope every single of my words
makes you feel something

me & coffee is a poetry collection about love, broken hearts, lost and found. this poetry collection captures the reality of a love life, a heavy reality story after the breakup. love poems for people who love someone, but don't end up together. a cup of coffee and blank paper such as a partner, helping to overcome emotions, the feelings deep within while waiting for the loved one to come home. but at some point, there comes a realization when time slaps with reality. time to let go of what has been lost and accepted that there is no way going back, but move on even though with a heavy heart. in the end, it's worth it.

dika agustin is an indonesian poet, she known as an instapoet. her works have been air on social media, and her genre poetry is narrative poetry. she wrote a lot of poems about love, life, personal growth, and such. in february, 2019 she published her debut poetry book: deep wounds. she hopes her writings can touch people's hearts and help people heal.

to continuous support and
stay connected with dika
or for more creative stuff
follow her on social media
@dikagustin

hello

have you finished read me & coffee?
the after-taste would mean a lot to me
so, would you mind to share
your experience through
amazon or goodreads?

Printed in Great Britain
by Amazon